CONTRIBUTORS

PHOTOGRAPHERS

Rob Durston
www.durstonphoto.com

Simon Mills
www.photosby.si

Connor Tilson
www.connortilson.com

Rebecca McMaster
*www.facebook.com/rebecca
mcmasterphotography*

Dalyce Wilson
dalycewilson@gmail.com

Tony Pleavin
www.tonypleavin.com

Terence Finnegan

Gavin Millar
www.gavinmillar.com

Sarah Bryden Photography
and Living Witness Productions

WRITERS

Jim Kitchen

Pádraig Ó Tuama

Jim Allen

James Orr

Chelsea Marshall

Jonathan Hobbs

Stephen Collins

Ben Craig

COPY EDITOR

Janet Davidson

KICKSTARTER VIDEO

Orlaith Wood

Simon Wood

Tim McCullough

Journeyfor
www.journeyfor.co.uk

EDITORIAL

We like Northern Ireland. We have always known it is full of people doing amazing things, but it is hard to start the day with our heads full of negative media about Northern Ireland, slowly but definitely seeping into our view of the world.

We are living in a time where consumerism seems to be valued higher than biodiversity, human rights, equality and human relationships. Scientists are calling for an 80% decrease in our carbon emissions by 2050, and it feels like we are not moving fast enough. Feeling this disempowered scares us. It is so enormous and lonely to own the problems of the world, and so tiny and lonely to be told all we can do is turn off the light switch. We - the Freckle team - disagree on what the answer to this is, but agree that the right sort of story can feel like a ray of sunlight on a dark day. We disagreed on lots of things ... cycling in the rain, goat burgers, politics. Whether to ask Liam Neeson to be on the front cover of the first issue. But we agree that the world needs more people doing what makes them feel alive, carving out their own stories.

We want to tell these positive stories, to practise slow journalism and find out what gets people out of bed. Stories of fresh air, home-grown vegetables and adventures in the Mournes. Making saris and sharing poetry. Weather-beaten, wintery beaches and sun off the waves on a morning surf. Building boats and rebuilding bikes. Knowing and remembering more about our landscapes and the hidden community gardens in our cities. Celebrating the people quietly creating art that echoes the beauty of our favourite places.

There are a thousand answers to what it looks like to live sustainably, peacefully and creatively. So here, now, we bring you the first issue of Freckle: a celebration, a tribute to our storytelling, to our people, our landscapes, our livelihoods and creativity. These are a collection of stories, a rough, crumbly mixture of styles and responses to the times we are living in. They do not come from a place of naive denial, they come from our need to just get up and do something. This issue looks at the themes of ocean, soil, belonging, expressing and exploring. Read slowly, read out loud around a campfire, read anywhere. Leave it on a park bench when you're done. Delve into the spirit of our times and discover what is really going on in Northern Ireland. Let us know what you think. Go slow, and celebrate. We hope you like it.

Lynn Finnegan

Freckle Team

OCEAN

People on the north coast can be fiercely loyal
to the ocean. It becomes a part of their life, their
wonderings and wanderings, their every day. We
meet some of them and explore what they do to
satisfy their ocean cravings.

VALKYRIE CRAFTS

photos by Rob Durston

John and Hamish Wilkinson, first and foremost practising canoeists,
are also artisans in wooden Canadian canoes and kayaks. They work
to build boats that last for more than a hundred years, look graceful
in the water and paddle beautifully.

The Wilkinsons' workshop sits on the hills above Castlerock on the north coast, on a clear day opening out to a view across to the shores of Islay and Jura of Scotland. From here you can start to understand the bygone days of the old Kingdom of Dál Riata that spanned western Scotland and north east Ulster. From a view like this you could be forgiven for thinking it is almost swimming distance between the two lands.

Step into the workshop and the smell of freshly-planed cedar and pine lift your spirits almost immediately, evoking images of vast Canadian forests and a time when native Canadian canoes were paddled and maintained for hundreds of years. And they still can be. A wooden Canadian canoe or sea kayak, if properly built and cared for, can last for more than a hundred years. John Wilkinson and his son Hamish build such wooden works of art, keeping alive the traditional art of boat building.

They are first and foremost practising canoeists, so they know how they want their boats to feel in the water. Their starting point for any boat is to measure your body height and the length of your limbs. The boat is built for you. Started as a hobby, by 2005 Valkyrie was in existence and John was focusing on cedar and canvas boats close in design to the American Indian birch bark canoe. They take between one and three months to make by hand, with steam-bent frames and hand-planed paddles.

Their name Valkyrie pays homage to the Norwegian influence in the 'drontheim' design, the traditional fishing boats found all along the north of Ireland. In Norwegian mythology Valkyries exist as beautiful swans, except in times of battle, when they take the slain heroes off the battle field and carry them to heaven. Valkyries, the Norwegian angels of death.

Hamish has been joining his dad for years in the workshop after school, and since finishing sixth year has joined John full time. Last summer he became resolute in his ambition to circumnavigate the island of Ireland. He built his own sea kayak for the trip, in an old gracefully streamlined West Greenland style. There's a different kayak for every type of water, but the Greenland kayak is one of the best designs in the world if you want to spend time at sea: it has evolved over thousands of years, is flatter, narrower and faster than a lot of its counterparts, and fares better in high winds. They modified it to carry all the kit and food needed, and Hamish set off clockwise around the country in late summer 2014.

The four main corners of Ireland – Torr Head, Carnsore Point, Mizen and Malin Head – were the real marking points of the journey. And his kayak did him proud. Because there are no screws in the design, the whole piece is held together by the structure which makes the whole thing quite flexible. Hamish said, "It kinda felt like it was alive, more like a living companion than a piece of equipment". It shifted and bent with the waves like no piece of plastic could. Which came in handy when he once dropped it on the beach and it bounced instead of broke. Hamish named it Selkie, a creature that comes up in stories and old songs throughout Ireland, Scotland and North America. They are said to live as seals at sea, but shed their skin to become human on land. Some reckon if traced carefully, most Selkies are based on Inuit hunters going off course and coming ashore along these coastlines. Hamish didn't encounter any on this particular adventure, but instead arrived home, windswept and wiser, seventy days later to become the youngest person to paddle solo around Ireland.

When asked if there was one thing they would like everyone to know about boats, they were in clear agreement: traditional systems and materials are just as viable as our modern plastic ways of living, and in many cases better. The knowledge systems and practices are living and flexible, just like the wooden kayak moves and shifts with the water beneath you. ●

explore more at: www.valkyriecraft.com

LOVE OF THIS SALTED FRINGE

photos by Rob Durston

Jim Allen leads walks and talks along the north coast, is the author of An Island's Treasure – Environmental Guide to North Coast Beaches, *designer of the current marine exhibition in Portrush Coastal Zone and has been Coleraine Borough Council's Environment Officer for the last twenty-five years. Jim's writings and paintings are inspired by the coast that is his home, and he can often be found playing about in traditional boats and wrecking for flotsam.*

Every now and again I would find myself standing somewhere on the northern coastline, facing the sea, happily mopping up the mood of the moment and trying to define just what it is about this place that never fails to exhilarate my senses and create within me such a sense of well-being. On one such occasion I sat in a grassy nook on the cliffs close to the Priest's Hole between Dunluce Castle and the Whiterocks, hidden from the road, and with a warm morning sun behind I took in the splendour of a smooth blue-green sea laid out below me. With the Portrush Skerries just off to my left, I looked out to where the Rhinns of Islay shimmered on the north-east horizon some thirty miles away and breathed deep, filling my lungs with warm air scented with a combination of dry, springy grass and placid seawater.

It was one of those occasional moments mysteriously allotted to mortals when time parks up in a viewpoint lay-by and patiently invites a response. At that moment, I was in a living picture whose frame extended from the immeasurable clear blue space above to an unending horizon beyond. Not far beneath my bum was a labyrinth of chalk caves, coves, sinkholes and creeks, battered, shattered, melted, gouged, pummelled and carved by a relentless and rhythmic Atlantic and all with beautiful nicknames like Sliddery, Cathedral, Ace of Spades, Long Gilbert and Benjamin's Port, each with its own peculiar history. I was aware of no other human frame within sight, hearing or thought. I saw no traffic save for a distant tanker to the west, anchored off Innishowen Head. I saw no buildings save for a small, rusty, red metal pinnacle, marking a reef east of the Skerries. A mark known as the Stookan (where we get the word for corn stook from) which my

〉〉

grandfather would be paid the princely sum of one florin by Irish Lights to row out every now and again and paint when tide and sea permitted. I saw no fences, borders, signs or flags. Hence perched alone and at ease, I realised that above all I was blessed to call this place home.

In my head I downloaded my favourite playlist of happy experiences and events associated with this coast and beyond to the Scottish Hebrides and I thought of the many friends that I had made through common circumstance and a love of this salted fringe. The depth of the space, the unique light and the endless motion of a chameleon sea that mimics the sky, all hanging like a favourite picture that repaints itself in different colours every day. I mouthed a tribute to my God.

I have worked, played, prayed and lived all of my fifty-five-year-old life along this famous island seaboard. I have maintained and campaigned, written about and sang about, sketched, painted, led walks, given talks, paddled, sailed, rowed and swam, leapt, wept, wrecked, inspected, collected, courted and reported, been impressed and distressed, been baptised and cried and almost died upon, and beside, this beguiling seaside, where wind and tide frustrate and fixate, dictate and create.

In this alpha and omega of habitats, where land and sea simultaneously begin and end, a million daily glass fists break and shake, hiss and kiss its northern shore. Here have come and gone invaders, raiders, scientists, poets, tourists, purists, surfers, sailors, hikers, bikers, photographers, cartographers, emigrants and immigrants, castle builders of stone and sand, second home developers of profit and land, fishers and crabbers, with rope and chain and lament and refrain. All drawn towards and cast about like a happy, dysfunctional company in a tangled time line of coastal dwellers inspired and shaped by sea and sand and rock.

On that day, within such a reflective bubble, memories blended with present feelings to cook up my allotted response to the ocean and this coastline. Out spilled words that I had learned and heard and spoke in a swell-like rhythm. From that day I forged my testimony to the seaside. •

GANNET, FULMAR, TERN 'n' AUK

Gannet, fulmar, tern 'n auk; skerry, creek, rhinn 'n rock.
Mark, mooring, buoy 'n chain; blown out dune 'n machair-plain.
Beach, strand, silt 'n sand; reef breaks 'n kittiwakes.
Storm, squall, splash 'n spray; port, point, arch 'n bay.

Cockle, cowrie, winkle, prawn; pool, light, sunset, dawn.
Hulls, gulls, keels 'n seals; bait, buckets, nets 'n creels.
Buckie, blenny, limpet, crab; rod, cod, bass 'n dab.
Wreck, ruin, weed 'n wrack; lee-ho, 'n gybe 'n tack.

Currach, drontheim, punt 'n boat; skimboard, kayak, sink 'n float.
Towline, throwline, life 'n limb; sinker, clinker, jump 'n swim.
Rollock, rudder, gunwhale, mast; hoist, 'n furl 'n make fast.
Cap 'n roll, plunge 'n spill; berms, worms, plankton, krill.

Stook, cliff, shelf 'n stack; spring, neap, rip 'n slack.
Eddy, gyre, wind 'n fetch; coble, drascombe, gaff 'n ketch.
Carrick, crag, coral, wave; chalk, flint, cove 'n cave.
Bale, sail, mizzen, stay; luff 'n trim 'n bear-away.

Tiller, helm, becket, sprit; ripple, cusp, shoal 'n spit.
Urchin, jelly, starfish, wrasse; thrift 'n spurge 'n scurvy grass.
Marram, mud, moths 'n flies; biscuit beaches, clear blue skies. Windbreaks,
castles, picnics, fun; ice cream, sun cream, too much sun.

Fairlead, hank, shackle, cleat; run 'n reach 'n broach 'n beat.
Puffins, pipits, paddles, props; dolphins, sharks 'n purple-tops.
Hook, line, catch 'n cast; reel, snag 'n hold-fast.
Starboard, stroke, bull 'n oar; regatta, race, 'n weather shore.

Tender, fender, anchor, chain; tie up, luff up, jib 'n main.
Lobster, scallop, salmon, trout; hard-a-lee 'n come about.
Shrimp, slater, rag 'n lug; flatties, dogs, sponge 'n slug.
Pontoons, jetties, walls 'n yawls; foghorn, oystercatcher calls.

Shingle, tangle, kelp 'n shell; onshore, offshore, alongshore, swell.
Flukes 'n fins 'n bones 'n stone; clams 'n claws 'n ice cream cones.
Sea-smooth, driftwood, coloured glass; an island's
    treasure none can surpass.
For we all love to be beside the lonely,
    busy, deep 'n wide, edgy, salty
    northern seaside.

Jim Allen

THE WELCOME ORGANISATION

photos by Rob Durston

---

*Francine, Sean, Julie-Anne, Gary and a crew of about ten people all spend
time at the Welcome Centre in Belfast. They can often be spotted with
Robbie Brennen, a volunteer at the centre, whose soul also happens to
belong to the ocean. He has spent time on and off Ireland's seas for decades.
One day at the Welcome Centre, hemmed in by four concrete walls, he said
to the crew, "Hey guys, how 'bout we build a boat?"*

"What d'you mean build a boat? What are you on about?"

"Yeah, come on, let's build a boat."

They thought he'd lost his marbles, but Robbie was determined and went on to wangle an old hull of a 17-foot Lough Foyle punt made from a one-hundred-year-old mould. The group managed to get access to a lock up unit near the Welcome Centre and started working on the boat two days a week. It slowly dawned on each of the crew that this could actually be possible. "And, I tell you ... it's been some craic," says Sean.

The Centre is a stalwart pillar of support in Belfast, each year helping around 1,300 people who are homeless or vulnerable. Along with the Centre's policy of no Celtic or Rangers tops, Robbie has three unwritten rules: no messing around, no drink and no drugs. Break any of those and you're out, but abide by them and it's mighty craic for everyone around. Julie-Anne, with her infectious smile, has become an expert in laying fibreglass, and the oars were made from

ash by Sean and Eamonn. Within a few months Robbie walked into a *Tree of Life* workshop one day and there were Francine and Julie-Anne being classroom assistants for a woodworking class with a special needs group. It has blown Robbie away.

Four months later, the boat was starting to look seaworthy. They named it *Lynne's Dream*, or *Aisling Lynn* in Irish, after a former employee of the Centre, Lynne McMordie. It launched to a huge crowd on the River Lagan during Easter week 2014 and the crew have since taken it to regattas on the River Bann and along the north coast.

Francine caught the first mackerel in the summer with homemade jigs, and they gutted and cooked it in the marina. The crew have also spent a summer night up on the north coast, launching three boats from Dunseverick and rowing with all their supplies to an old fisherman's cottage squeezed at the bottom of a cliff at Port Moon. With no electricity or running water, dinner was served up on a wood burning stove by candlelight,

Julie-Anne at the rudder.

before a night outside in sleeping bags under the stars. "Fecking brilliant," says Sean and Francine. "I haven't laughed so much in my life. It's like we didn't have a care in the world, and we didn't ... once we got on that minibus out of Belfast we forgot about them."

The boat crew are still around the Welcome Centre, and will not hear a word against it. They say *Lynne's Dream* has given them confidence and made them even tighter as a group, but most of all it is the Welcome Centre that allowed it to happen. It is there for everyone who needs it. Around 22,000 people a year present as homeless in Northern Ireland, and face almost constant daily experiences where they are made to feel isolated or vulnerable. "When you come in here they make you feel like you are somebody. You have a voice," says Francine. It feels like one big family, with all the merciless slagging and tough love that comes with the best of Northern Irish family life.

It is clear that Robbie and Ali (his wife) go that extra mile for the crew, and in the Autumn Julie-Anne nominated Robbie for the Credit Union's Volunteer of the Year Award. The first Robbie knew of it was an invitation in the post telling him to turn up at the Balmoral Hotel, and on the night, he won it. Robbie insists that it is only with the continued help and support from Rob Ruddock and Paul Brannigan from Bushmills and the Welcome management team that the crew have been able to experience these amazing adventures. And they have just been gifted another boat from the Isle of Islay – more work to be done, and craic to be had.

Lynne's dream, *Aisling Lynne*, flies the flag of the Causeway Coast Maritime Heritage Club; a square flag with green and blue triangles meeting in the middle to signify blue sea and sky meeting green fields from both sides of the border. Watch closely for the square flag on the boats you pass in the water: it could be the Welcome crew. •

Robbie Brennen

explore more at: www.homelessbelfast.org

SOIL

"If we want to evaluate how well we love ourselves, others and the Earth, there is no better barometer than how we grow and eat food. With food, fundamental questions about how we live our lives and organise our societies are literally in your face."

(David Gee, 2012)

Look closely, and you can begin to see the ripples of people cultivating both food and community in various corners of Northern Ireland, bringing people together and closer to the food we eat and the land it comes from.

words by Jim Kitchen

'Grown here, not flown here' – that's one of the snappy slogans for Northern Ireland's food. Like all the best advertising, it captures in five words the story behind the high-quality produce that underpins Belfast's culinary metamorphosis.

In the past few years, it's been transformed; a city dismissed as a gastronomic backwater for so long is now being lauded by the critics who flock to dine at Ox and Shu, visit St George's Market or pay homage at The Arcadia. And so they should; every award earned by these Belfast businesses has been well deserved and long overdue.

Today's celebrated restaurateurs would be quick to acknowledge their debt to Nick Price, whose Cathedral Quarter bistro lit up a part of the city that didn't even know it had a Quarter. His menu was based on simple, honest and local ingredients. He knew good food needs good soil. Around the same time, John McCormick was taking his first steps in growing organic vegetables.

THE ORGANIC GROWER

photos by Simon Mills

The early years of the organic movement in Ireland were dominated by 'blow-ins', mostly migrants from England or Europe who wanted to live as close to self-sufficiency as possible. Many were inspired by John Seymour, the acclaimed author of *The Complete Book of Self-Sufficiency*, then living in Wexford. They organised festivals like The Mustard Seed Gathering where they learned from each other, shared experiences and spread their ideas.

Among them was a young John McCormick, then a budding horticultural scientist. He'd already acquired an enthusiastic interest in organic production methods during a placement at one of the Camphill communities and, despite the lack of enthusiasm that he encountered among his peers, John's path had been set.

He came to work within another Camphill community in Kilkeel and, later, as the Farm Manager at the Ulster Folk Museum. Those years built the experience – often learning from his mistakes – that prepared John for the leap of faith that propelled him into his own venture in 1991 – Helen's Bay Organic Gardens.

John became the first commercial organic vegetable grower in Northern Ireland. He supplied a few restaurants and sold his produce at Bangor's weekly market for the first two years. Then he started his box scheme. He'd seen them working in Holland and Germany; now he decided to test the model here.

Starting with ten customers, the box scheme has become the backbone of the business, with three hundred and thirty households now supplied each week. The principle is simple enough – a customer receives a weekly order of fruit and vegetables, based on seasonal availability – in other words, whatever John is harvesting in any particular week, supplemented with organic produce from some partner farms.

John's passionate commitment to organic farming is at the core of his business. "It's the food that I wanted to provide for my own children and many of my customers share that desire," he says. "Organic standards ensure that our produce is healthy and safe, grown without chemicals and pesticides, free from any GM content and, crucially,

maintaining a natural, fertile soil. We have to pass a rigorous inspection each year that is our guarantee of organic status."

John's customers also value the fact that the produce is local. Of course, it's not yet possible to grow bananas in Co. Down (although, with climate change, who knows what might happen in fifty years?) so some fruit and veg, always organic, is brought in to supplement what is grown in the fields and polytunnels at Helen's Bay. Over the year, about 65% of the produce is local and John thinks he can get that figure up to 75%.

He both laughs and despairs at the 'can't do' philosophy around here. When he started out twenty three years ago, he remembers a neighbour coming around and saying, "aye, you can plough the land, but you'll never grow organic vegetables." At harvest, he came around again, saw the vegetables growing carefree and abundant, and said, "aye, you can grow organic vegetables, but you'll never sell them." "What is it with the 'you can't do' attitude?" John asks. That kind of response to new things can feel poisonous, it can ground people down and ultimately become a big obstacle to social and economic development.

John's a pioneer, always has been. He's chosen that 'road less travelled' because he's a man of principle, with strong ethical values and an undiminished visionary passion for the job he always wanted. He is certainly one of Northern Ireland's most influential champions of sustainable food, probably its first. Now, two brothers from Ballycastle are part of a new wave of producers who are informed by the same principles.   >>

THE KID BROTHERS

photos by Simon Mills

Goat's cheese dishes are a staple of most restaurant menus these days and demand for the product has been growing steadily over the past few years. That's good news for the goat dairy industry but it creates a waste stream that has been overlooked by most people.

Only she-goats are of any use to a dairy farmer – the billies (male goats) are slaughtered shortly after they're born because it's too costly, too labour-intensive, to rear them in most commercial enterprises. In the UK, that amounts to around thirty thousand male goats despatched in this way every year.

Now, Charlie and Sandy Cole – the Kid Brothers of Broughgammon Farm – are tackling this challenge head-on.

The brothers returned to the fifty-acre family farm above Ballycastle, having acquired complementary skills in rural management and catering during their college years.

Fuelled by the confidence of youth and a fierce determination to succeed, their first idea was to raise wild boar on the farm (and they still might, in a few years' time) but eventually settled on raising goat kids for their meat.

However, the customers weren't immediately queuing up to buy this cabrito, the much more elegant Spanish name for the goat-kid meat, so the boys went 'on the road'.

Their fresh meat stall is now a familiar sight at farmers' markets around the province – in Comber, Newtownbreda, Larne, Derry and beyond, with a regular slot at St George's Market on Sundays.

Meanwhile, their catering operation features prominently at the many events organised by Food NI throughout the year. The charismatic brothers can be found cooking up their wonderfully-named Billy Burgers and Cabrito Burritos at festivals from Balmoral to Ballymaloe.

They've started growing their own vegetables for their catering and, to complete the local sourcing, they get their bread rolls from Donnelly's bakery in Ballycastle, so you'll be hard pressed to find a more sustainable offering than Broughgammon's Billy Burger.

Goats may be mankind's earliest domesticated animal and eaten all around the world but it has more or less disappeared from most Irish plates. Yet, there are lots of good reasons to choose cabrito – it's lean, low-calorie and really tasty but it's also local, sustainable and ethical.

Broughgammon's barns are brimming with around three hundred kids, with plans to expand the herd and the housing over the next year.

And it's not just goats on the farm.

Applying the same principles that led them to the goats in the first place, they've also acquired a small herd of male calves from neighbouring dairy farms. As with goats, so it is with male calves – they're of no commercial use, which condemns over one hundred thousand male dairy calves to slaughter within hours of their birth in the UK.

The calves are reared outdoors to produce free-range rose veal. It's a niche market, one that hasn't yet been able to overcome the reputation earned by the use of the now-banned veal crates. These calves are far

>>

" Goats may be mankind's earliest domesticated animal and eaten all around the world but it has more or less disappeared from most Irish plates. Yet, there are lots of good reasons to choose cabrito "

removed from that notorious practice; they live longer and better lives than many farm animals.

They've also moved into supplying some seasonal wild game, including wild venison, duck, pheasant and are always on the lookout for wild rabbit, all sourced from responsible, licensed hunters. They've also added a series of dried locally-picked seaweeds to their suite of Broughgammon products.

The Coles' ethical and sustainable stance on meat production informs every aspect of the farm's operation. They've already won awards for their environmental improvement scheme, their water management and their use of renewable energy technologies but it's their enthusiasm and innovation that leaves a lasting impression.

Charlie and Sandy Cole are an inspiration. With the considerable support of their family, they're developing a great business on a small family farm with skill and passion.

THE CHANGE MAKER

photos by Rob Durston

A different business model underlies Eileen Wilson's work but it is infused with the same skill and passion. Eileen manages a Sustainable Living programme at the Footprints Women's Centre, which provides support services for women and children in the Colin Neighbourhood.

Footprints operates as a social enterprise, with its trading arm providing a significant proportion of the Centre's funding. It has developed a strong ethos of self-help, created employment in the heart of a disadvantaged community, building skills and self-confidence.

The daily reality of food poverty touches many in the Colin district. There is a high level of disadvantage, significantly greater than in most other parts of Northern Ireland's cities. And it's here that Eileen and her team have been transforming the food culture of the area beyond recognition.

For more than a decade, the Centre has been fostering initiatives on healthy food. Its involvement had its genesis in the provision of low-cost meals to a hundred women and seventy children every day at its drop-in centre. That developed into an innovative social economy enterprise, providing a delivery service to some seventy community organisations and businesses.

In 2002, a project to promote healthy living identified the local barriers to good food choices, noting the limited access to high quality, reasonably priced food, especially fruit and vegetables. This work laid the foundations of a new policy, aimed at tackling health inequalities through the provision of sustainable and healthy food.

So far, so strategic. But where this project has really made a difference is in teaching

women in the community a whole new set of life-skills. By offering practical cooking sessions, lessons on budgeting and shopping, food safety and nutrition, the Centre has responded to the needs of its target groups, ranging from young mothers to senior citizens.

Taster sessions provide new food experiences; dishes prepared in the Centre get taken home; self-cooked dishes like mince pies are compared with their pale processed imitations – all part of a revitalised culinary education in a safe and socially enriching environment to support Footprints' commitment to providing healthy eating at affordable prices.

Now, it's adding the skills of growing food. In a three-year project drawing its inspiration from the Transition Towns movement, the Centre has transformed an overgrown, neglected space within their grounds by creating raised beds, fruit trees and herb gardens. Last year twenty-five women and twenty children learned new skills under the instruction of an experienced local gardener. Angela, Irene and Maureen are part of a new growing group who have one season under their belt, but say they wouldn't miss it for the world. What they've also realised is that you don't need that much space to grow and nurture plants. And if you have no space at all, you'd be surprised how many strawberries you can get from a hanging basket. Their kids are now out checking the pea plants more than once a day to see if they've grown.

Their kitchen garden, managed by their volunteers, supplies many of the fresh ingredients for the Centre's catering, including the meals for children in the day-care facility and the on-site cafe. In addition, the kitchen uses produce diverted

from landfill through the charity, Fareshare, to prepare meals. Over the past five years, Footprints' work on food, nutrition and physical activity has reached two thousand people in the Colin Neighbourhood.

Eileen has led the initiative and extended its reach into other aspects of sustainable living – the Centre composts its green waste, recycles and reuses all relevant materials and reduces its carbon emissions through the recent installation of solar electric and solar hot-water panels.

This multi-dimensional approach has led to national recognition – the best Community and Sustainability project in the UK's Cultivation Street competition 2014, following the regional winner for Northern Ireland of The Conservation Foundation's Gardening Against the Odds award in 2012.   ≫

THE VILLAGE PEOPLE

photos by Simon Mills

Away from the city, Cloughmills is a much smaller rural community in Co. Antrim facing its own social problems of anti-social behavior, apathy and disadvantage. Like so many villages, Cloughmills has lost many of its traditional skills, and with it people have lost that close connection to their soil and landscapes. With the same inspirational spirit of self-help that Eileen has, Patrick Frew has led a team of volunteers to reconnect people with each other, their community and their natural environment using the language of food.

It started off with an idea to get young people off the streets: together with a small group, Patrick transformed a small plot of derelict land beside the main street pub; the neglected scrubland of 2009 became an attractive and productive vegetable garden a year later. In return for giving collected food to elderly people in the village, the young people got points that earned them trips to go camping, coasteering, fishing and canoeing.

From these humble beginnings, the village has been stirred into spectacular action over the last five years and has become universally known as Incredible Edible Cloughmills.

The experience they gained was put to further productive use when the group acquired almost five acres of land on an old mill site – this has become the locus for most of the campaign's activities. The area now houses two polytunnels, an extensive vegetable garden and a newly-established orchard, but that's the tip of the activity iceberg.

" Last year they got closer to their goal of transforming the village into an edible landscape: apple trees planted in people's gardens were cultivated, and spare apples were brought to the community-owned apple press. "

The Cloughmills team has harnessed its enviable energy and creativity to take this community development well beyond a mere growing project. It works with primary school children and those who left school more years ago than they care to remember to collaborate on a dizzying array of food initiatives.

If you'd like to learn how to make jam or chutney, bake bread or forage for wild foods, there's a class for that. Create your

>>

own pizza from scratch, understand the healing properties of food, learn what to feed your toddler – yes, there's a class for that, too.

Last year they got closer to their goal of transforming the village into an edible landscape: apple trees planted in people's gardens were cultivated, and spare apples were brought to the community owned apple press. The softer skills of inter-generational understanding and caring for your community are as important as the knowledge around cultivating food.

The processes of learning valuable new skills and the potential for generating new micro-businesses have been a vital part of the project – this is real community development, abundantly visible and enormously successful. Incredible Edible Cloughmills has become a tourist destination in its own right, with visitors coming to see what all the fuss is about from as far away as Finland and Estonia. It's been recognised, too, by its rapidly expanding clutch of awards.

These are projects led by people who are not likely to feature in the 'foodie' literature but their contribution to Northern Ireland's food renaissance is no less important than the 'headline' acts. John, the Cole brothers, Eileen and Patrick each bring to their work all the passion and proficiency of the true enthusiast. They're part of what might be called a non-aligned movement; independently of each other, they're involved in connecting people more fully with what they eat, and are driven by the power of food to drive positive change in their communities. ●

explore more at:

www.helensbayorganicgardens.com
www.broughgammon.com
www.footprintswomenscentre.org
www.cloughmills.org.uk

Jim Kitchen is from Belfast Food Network, working for a healthy, local and seasonal food system in Northern Ireland:

www.belfastfoodnetwork.org

BELONGING

"Society, as we have constituted it, will have no place
for me, has none to offer; but Nature, whose sweet rains
fall on unjust and just alike, will have clefts in the rocks
where I may hide, and secret valleys in whose silence
I may weep undisturbed. She will hang the night with
stars so that I may walk abroad in the darkness without
stumbling, and send the wind over my footprints so that
none may track me to my hurt: she will cleanse me in
great waters, and with bitter herbs make me whole."

Oscar Wilde, *De Profundis*

THE HIDDEN GEM

photos and words by Dalyce Wilson

Among Belfast's cultural groups, a hidden gem can be found in ArtsEkta, an arts and cultural organisation that works to develop intercultural relationships at the heart of the community. Ekta means bonding, or unity, in Hindi, and you can see this strand of belonging woven through their many projects.

I had the wonderful opportunity to meet with a project facilitator for ArtsEkta, Karishma Kusurkar, who is currently facilitating a community endeavour called the Sari Project. "The Sari Project teaches people from both the Indian subcontinent and elsewhere about the traditional Sari. Participants work to create a brand new Sari that will be block printed onto fabrics at the end of the project," explains Karishma. Getting involved is completely free and is based over seven weeks. The finished product will be a large Sari comprised of the prints and textiles that all of the participants have created, and will be displayed in a local gallery.

"One class focuses on discussing symbolism with the Saris. Later participants will bring along objects that mean something personal to them. These personal belongings will be integrated in the sketches, drawings and designs of the Saris." The cultural significance of the Sari is explored throughout the project. "I don't think many people realise that most Saris expose the belly," explains Karishma, "or that they don't necessarily have religious significance".

According to Karishma, the Sari Project aims to celebrate and explore the rich Indian culture and heritage with people here in Northern Ireland and beyond. "I think some people have in their head a stereotype of the Indian people. The Sari Project allows participants to ask questions about India, the country, culture and its people. Projects like ours are helping to bridge the gap between our cultures: to share what we have in common, to share cultures between the indigenous people of Northern Ireland and the people of India and South Asia." Organisations like ArtsEkta help to integrate people from non-White European cultures into mainstream society here in Northern Ireland, alongside sharing, educating and creating ethnic artwork and meaning.

ArtsEkta also have a larger heritage project called Sanskriti, a new long-term endeavour that has been three years in the works. Rachel Radcliffe, the current Project Manager, is looking forward to the project investigating trade, cultural practice, migration and rights of passage. It's a shared heritage project that focuses on

>>

history and people's experiences, but it's also about creating a lovely product and creating stories that are accessible to other people as well. "In the end there will be a big archive of audio and written material for the public to access," says Karishma. "Many of these projects involve weaving in local stories and symbols with Indian culture and imagery. To successfully combine the two is quite difficult, but the women in the group have done a great job of exploring and treasuring both local and Indian culture."

Along with the Sari Project, ArtsEkta organises one of the biggest cultural events of the year in Northern Ireland: the Belfast Mela. Mela is a Sanskrit word meaning 'to meet', and is used in the Indian subcontinent for gatherings of all sizes. Although Melas traditionally have a strong south-Asian focus, ArtsEkta have adopted the concept with a broad multi-cultural focus, creating a festival that promotes an impressive array of cultures through the arts. Inspired by local and international talent, the programme celebrates identity through music, dance, food and visual arts. And people can't get enough: the festival has grown in size, with annual audiences increasing from 5,000 to 30,000 since 2007. Like ArtsEkta, Mela is an artistically-led celebration of culture and creativity. •

explore more at: www.artsekta.org.uk

THE BAKERS

Dara and Ciara OhArtghaile
Ursa Minor Bakery, Ballycastle

photos by Simon Mills   *words by Stephen Collins*

Having only learnt how to make bread in the past couple of years, Dara and Ciara OhArtghaile were unlikely candidates to become full-time bakers. "I still can't really believe that I make bread, and people come to buy my bread," utters Dara with genuine surprise etched across his fantastically-bearded face. "It's weird to imagine that people I've never met may currently be enjoying my bread. Growing up, I would never have imagined becoming a baker. I guess I just found something I love to do."

Married in summer 2013, the young couple have had a hectic year with the arrival of their first child, Cillian. Even so, their brimming enthusiasm is clear to see when it comes to talking about home-made, 'real' bread. "The idea came from when we were travelling in New Zealand," Dara continues. "The café culture over there is amazing. It's not 'chainy'. They're all very independent, and they all source and supply themselves. They're self-sustainable, baking their own breads and treats, and that was something we didn't really see happening here in Northern Ireland."

Ursa Minor Bakery (Latin name for the constellation, Little Bear) was formed in February 2014 and still operates out of the OhArtghailes' kitchen on North Street in Ballycastle, now using 16kg bags of flour every couple of days. "It was so heart-warming when we went onto social media to tell people we were setting up an artisan bakery," explains Dara. "Within one day of putting ourselves on Facebook,

we'd gathered over six hundred likes. It was a real confirmation that people were genuinely interested."

"Because we weren't sure at the start that people were interested," adds Ciara. "A lot of people don't understand the concept of real, fresh bread, and neither did we at the beginning. They don't understand that it's only fresh that day, and that it's slightly more expensive because of all the work that goes into it and the high quality organic flour we use. We weren't sure if people would grasp what we were about."

Frustration at the countless chemical additives thrown into everyday loaves is another factor in why the couple are so desperate to succeed. "I don't think we were even aware of all the nonsense that goes into bread," says Ciara. "Even fancier breads that supermarkets bring out to try and convince people that they're eating well – they're still bulked up with sugar and additives, ultimately still giving us chemically-produced bread."

Dara nods in agreement, and highlights that the bread people are consuming may be damaging their health too, "If you buy a white pan loaf from a supermarket, you can almost inhale it. You basically swallow it whole, leaving you feeling really bloated. With our bread, you can't do that – you have to chew it."

Staying up baking in the kitchen until late every night, Dara only falls into bed after completing his morning deliveries. "The

>>

method I use can be traced back to the French bakers of the 1700s. These guys would have had a pig's trough essentially, and would have mixed their dough in there, before folding it from one side all the way down to the other. What they were doing was trapping air into the dough. And we replicate that on a small scale. It gives the bread a light, 'open' texture."

Having already demolished two delicious raspberry and almond friands in their company, it was clear to me that they are very good at their craft. And it's evident I am not the only one who has fallen under their spell. As hype continues to spread about Ursa Minor's produce, what are the big goals for the future? "I'd love us to have our own place one day," says Dara. "I think that would be the dream. Not exactly a big place, maybe a small café, doing mostly takeaways, with enough space to seat eight to ten people." However, this dream isn't his ultimate priority. "I just want to be known as a baker. I want people to say, 'Ah look, there's Dara the baker.' I think that's such a nice relationship for people in a town to have with their suppliers. I want people to feel free to ask any questions about our bread. And if I don't know the answer straight off, I'll find it."

"It's been great to see that there are an increasing number of artisan people in our food culture, who are looking to do something different, but something traditional. I think it's a really good time to be here on the north coast, and in Northern Ireland, where people are looking for change." •

> " I want people to say, 'Ah look, there's Dara the baker.' I think that's such a nice relationship for people in a town to have with their suppliers. "

explore more at: www.ursaminorbakery.co.uk

THE COMMUNITY WORKER

photos by Connor Tilson
words by Chelsea Marshall

Formerly a history teacher in Lithuania, Lina Zeimiene has clearly found her passion supporting migrant families to feel a sense of belonging in Northern Ireland. "Maybe in a life, every person gets what she wants, what she can do best. I'm not saying that I do best, but I like best this job and I'm very happy."

It's a cool Saturday morning, and the heavy rain has subsided by the time my bus pulls into Dungannon station. Lina Zeimiene is standing outside waiting to gather me into her car, and as her husband drives off, I squeeze into the back seat with two of her grandchildren.

Lina coordinates Language Club for the South Tyrone Empowerment Programme (STEP), and she is pleased but unsurprised to see nearly full attendance in the classes after a two-week break. More than one hundred and sixty children are gathered at the Willow Bank Community Centre,

>>

in classrooms designed for fewer, and Lina is looking forward to a much-needed expansion soon. She introduces me to each class of children aged six to twelve, engaged in a variety of lessons aimed at helping them gain confidence in the language of their parents and grandparents through understanding more about their cultural identity. Many of the children were born in Northern Ireland, so gathering to practice writing letters, locating hometowns on maps and learning the national anthem of their families' countries supports their ability to 'belong' in the widest sense.

> " [Lina] epitomises the person who can call everywhere home without losing a core identity of knowing where her journey started and how it shapes her world. "

Language Club began with twelve pupils in 2006 and now includes one hundred and sixty seven bilingual children in Lithuanian, Polish, Portuguese and Russian classes. Each week, children take part in language, history and culture lessons designed to help them maintain fluency in their first language, learn about local culture and build confidence in their cultural identity by actively participating in their community. Lina is quick to emphasise that the consistent and growing attendance in Language Club shows the interest children and their parents have in the space in which to cultivate linguistic confidence and nurture cultural identity. Although participation is nearly free to families, Lina explains the high value placed on the service: "Traditions, culture, language, life –

it's very expensive. You can't buy it. There's not enough money to buy all culture, all language."

Formerly a history teacher in Lithuania, Lina has clearly found her passion supporting migrant families to feel a sense of belonging in Northern Ireland. "Maybe in a life, every person gets what she wants, what she can do best. I'm not saying that I do best, but I like best this job and I'm very happy." Lina became one of the first Language Club teachers when she enrolled two of her grandchildren. Since then, she has become the coordinator of Language Club and a community support worker with STEP and BELONG, a programme that aims to promote a sense of belonging for black and minority ethnic children in Northern Ireland communities, schools and society. Bernadette McAliskey, STEP coordinator, describes Lina as "the centre of her extended family" and someone who "epitomises the person who can call everywhere home without losing a core identity of knowing where her journey started and how it shapes her world".

Despite her enthusiasm for the role, Lina also conveys the challenges of hearing and supporting families through the difficult experiences that many migrant workers face. She recognises language as the main barrier for adults finding a space within communities, and her work with Language Club is rooted in the belief that cultural and linguistic confidence is key to 'belonging'. The Club teaches children about their "own culture, and about this country, and this country's traditions. Children must know more about both cultures ... Our children must know who they are, from where they are, and remember that diversity in a community is very nice."

Reflecting on her own experience, Lina notes, "If I want to be myself, I must belong to two communities now: local and Lithuanian." •

THE GIANT

words by Thomas Muinzer

"The wonderful Irish Giant … is the most extraordinary curiosity ever known, or ever heard of in history; and the curious in all countries where he has been shewn, pronounce him to be the finest display of Human Nature they ever saw."

Morning Herald Newspaper, London, July 17, 1782

Whilst many readers may know that the Georgian period roughly spans the 1700s through to the early 1800s, fewer will know that one of the most remarkable and dramatic of Northern Irish stories occurred during this era. That story is the life of Derry's Charles Byrne, who was born in rural County Derry in 1761 and grew up in a small hamlet called Littlebridge. The Littlebridge of Charles' youth is now long gone, for the more sizeable town of Drummullan has sprouted where it once stood. Yet the Northern Irish landscape still gives a firm historical nod to these bygone days: the people of Drummullan townland still travel the 'Littlebridge Road', and the 'little' bridge from which Charles' home took its name remains.

Born into rural Derry's peasant class, Charles was soon marked out by nature for a life of fame and adventure. From a young age he began to grow rapidly, reaching such a prodigious height by his teen years that his renown spread across the land. Presently he was the subject of invitations to Springhill House, the elegant stately home in the area, where the young 'giant' was received by Derry's social finery.

By his late teens, Charles had decided to set off for the British mainland in pursuit of fame and fortune. Landing first in Scotland, he became an instant success. As Eric Cubbage has recounted, Edinburgh's "night watchmen were amazed at the sight of him lighting his pipe from one of the streetlamps on North Bridge without even standing on tiptoe." His celebrity spread as he made his way down through northern England, arriving in London in early 1782, aged twenty-one. Here he entertained paying audiences at rooms in Spring Garden-gate, then Piccadilly and Charing Cross. His gentle, likeable nature inspired an immense public fondness, and his celebrity life was constantly splashed across the newspapers of the day. By mid-1782, he had inspired a hit London stage show called *Harlequin Teague*, or *The Giant's Causeway*.

Unfortunately, Charles' height was the result of a then-undiscovered growth condition (known today as 'acromegalic gigantism'), and his health presently began to decline sharply in his twenty-second year. He was also pickpocketed in this period while drinking in his local pub, the Black Horse; Charles' worldly earnings were on his person in the form of banknotes, and were

>>

stolen. The loss of his earnings combined with his failing health, and two months later Charles passed away at his lodgings in June 1783, aged twenty-two.

Although Charles had made arrangements for his body to be buried at sea, his corpse was stolen on the way to his funeral by a crooked surgeon named John Hunter. Hunter studied Charles' remains and subsequently put his skeleton on display. It remains on display to this day in Hunter's memorial museum, the Hunterian Museum in London. However, Derry's beloved son may yet make a return to his homeland in order to be laid to rest, for in a letter in May last year, the Mayor of Derry at the time, Martin Reilly, wrote to the Museum's trustees advocating for "the importance of respecting the wishes of Mr Byrne in relation to his burial".

The final episode in the Derryman's remarkable story, then, may yet remain to be written … ●

LEFT: 'John Hunter': Portrait by John Jackson, © National Portrait Gallery, London. Part of Byrne's enormous skeleton can be seen in the top right corner.

PREVIOUS: 'Charles Byrne and Others': An etching of Byrne, seen here towering over his comrades. By his contemporary John Kay (1742-1826), © National Portrait Gallery, London.

THE CITIZENS FOR NATURE

Reflections on the power of saying 'no', understanding we are nothing without the land, air, water and the other intangible things that unite us.

words by James Orr

"Another world is not only possible,
she is on her way.
On a quiet day, I can hear her breathing."

Arundhati Roy

The voices of creative dissent are strong; they are determined, and they belong to a brooding quiet revolution of citizen action which is far beyond the grip of starker politics. The roots of this non-conforming tradition tap deep into rich seams of old and new thinking as varied as the landscapes they come from.

What if we don't want to belong to the institutions around us? The sterile systems and economic models that build cages of fear around us, denying the things we love because they do not have an economic value. More to do with 'not in my name' than 'not an inch', the dignity of the dissenter is their identity; their flag bears witness to the richness and simplicity of the ordinary, the understated and what we hold in common. The 'power of no' gets you off the treadmill, gets you listening to your heart – but more than anything, it is about belonging. The 'power of no' lives in a political courage that understands we are nothing without the land, air and water. It intuitively recognises that when we throw things away there is no such place as away.

Bill Donnelly has been saying 'no' to a gold mine near his home in Omagh and after years of relentless effort he remains a tower of strength. "The gold mine was first applied for on my 39th birthday. I'm now sixty and it's my wedding anniversary tonight. Before I go out for dinner I am firing off another objection to the latest underground mine proposal."

His tenacity is born out of a desire to protect his business from a mining operation that had his community "imprisoned in their homes". He is appalled at the systemic and persistent failure in enforcement from a system that did not seem to care. Bill simply says, "we're stopping this".

This is not saying 'no' for the sake of saying 'no' by the perfect or the petulant. Having the courage to see through what you want to see happen challenges us in a creative way: 'your truth is not my truth'. »

But it goes much further. It has an honesty about the problems we face that protects us from the abuse of others. The power of saying 'no' also shows that civil resistance works. From Rathlin to Fermanagh fracking companies are running scared. Zero Waste North West stopped a £750-million incinerator in Derry because they wanted cleaner air. The Loughshore Residents Association saved their public park in north Belfast from the predations of WalMart and Belfast City Council. 'No Creevy Quarry' is a campaign near Hillsborough aimed at protecting homes and their equestrian business from being dug up and sold onto China or London as aggregates. They will most likely win.

Anti-fracking campaigner Dawn Patterson is a mother, serial networker and teacher.

"There's nothing highfallutin about what I do … I just ask myself a question: why are we destroying this place and leaving a horrible legacy behind us? Common-sense solutions are not being applied. This is all fixable and doable and it's not getting fixed. I started because no one else is doing it but now I know others can be relied on when we need them."

To say 'no' reveals and affirms the strength of personal responsibility and what we can achieve in a collective way. If democracy is dying in Northern Ireland it is the creative dissenters who are helping nurse it back to life. These are voices from another world that may be on its way. •

EXPRESSING

"It doesn't interest me how old you are. I want to know if you will risk looking like a fool for love, for your dream, for the adventure of being alive.

...

It doesn't interest me where or what or with whom you have studied. I want to know what sustains you from the inside when all else falls away."

from *The Invitation*, Oriah Mountain Dreamer

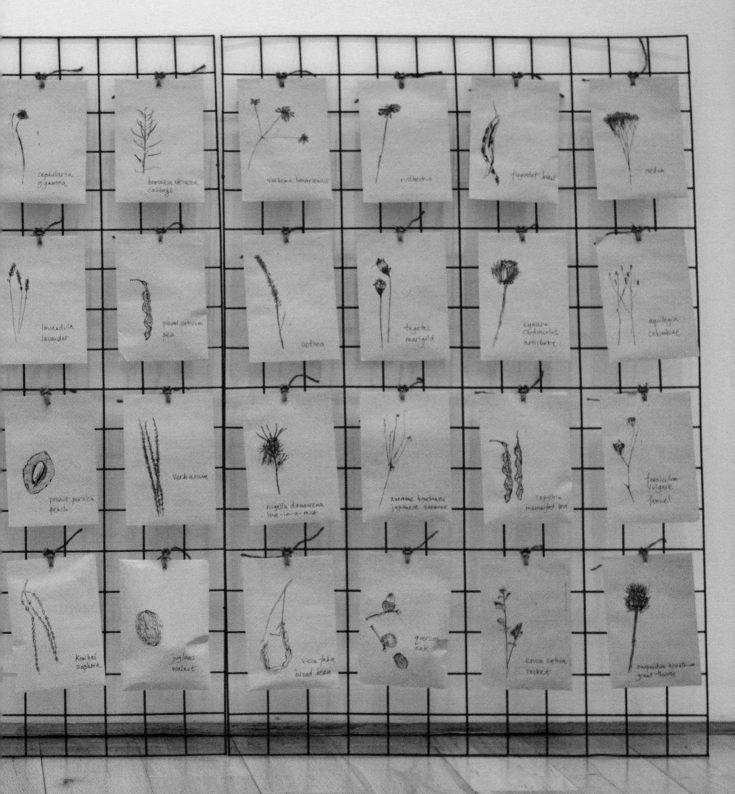

Alice Clark's *Dispersal* show at Armagh Market Place Gallery, Spring 2014
photo: Jordan Hutchings

ALICE CLARK

photos and words by
Hannah Armstrong

Alice Clark is an artist based in south Belfast. She uses natural materials sourced from the local environment to explore personal and collective relationships to the land, inviting audiences to engage in the conversation about how we live. Here she talks to Freckle *about her growth as an artist and planting seeds for the future.*

How did your journey as an artist begin?

Well, I was a weaver long before I became an artist – I studied and taught weaving for a long time. I did A Level Art while I was still weaving, and then I did a Degree in Fine Art at the University of Ulster. It opened up a whole new world of expression – the doors opened for me to make contemporary artwork, and I found it very exciting, very liberating.

How did your style develop to what it is today?

I had thought I wanted to be a painter, but my tutors at the Art College told me to take this opportunity to explore what the whole visual arts culture is. I've always been interested in trees and I was using paint to make linear marks like branches and trees and things like that. It was then, I suppose, they said, "Why don't you use the actual material rather than paint when trying to represent a tree?" Now I use the actual materials, whether it be plants or seeds, the earth or clay.

Where do you go to find inspiration and materials to work with?

I do quite a lot of picking stuff up when I find it along the way. The River Lagan is a wonderful space coming right out of the city centre, and it's possible to walk or cycle along it for ten miles or so. I like the fact that it's not over-managed – if a tree is fallen down it's left there to rot. During my Masters show I found these amazing giant hogweed plants which are eight foot high – I didn't know what they were exactly, but they had the most wonderful texture and these beautiful seed heads, like an enormous dandelion.

Your recent show in Armagh, Dispersal, *invited visitors to take part in a 'seed and story exchange'. Can you tell us more about it?*

Dispersal was about involving the audience in a dialogue about growing. I had asked people in advance to send me seeds and a story about those seeds, and during the exhibition new people brought their seeds and stories and exchanged them for those

>>

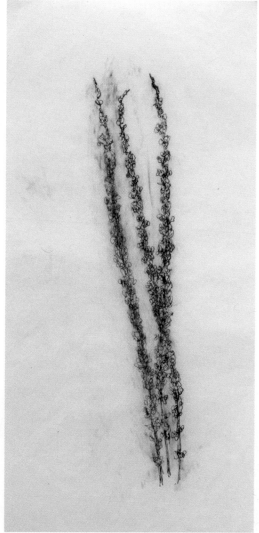

photos: Jordan Hutchings

of another. I had made drawings of the seed heads on brown paper envelopes, and inside the envelopes were the stories and seeds. I'd like to show the work again, maybe in the Botanic Gardens; it would feel fitting to move away from white cubic galleries and towards spaces where people will engage in a political way.

What are you working on at the moment?

In a show I had a year ago in Derry, I had a collection of small trees – saplings, about five or six feet in size. I want to liberate these trees – I want to invite an audience to go and plant one of my trees and to document their planting. What I'm interested in is greening up the environment. In the city centre there's very little green space, yet it is the oxygen of the city both in a literal sense and also for our mental well-being.

I've started a shared drawing project with two artist friends, one in Edinburgh and one in New Zealand. We've made two 'landscape' and 'mapping' themed sketchbooks out of scraps of paper and pages of old maps, and are posting them to each other intermittently. What I like about the project is that you're sharing your drawing, responding to the others' work and working upon each other's ideas. You just don't know what comes out of it, which is fun. It's all about trying things out, isn't it? That's what life's about. •

HANNAH COATES

photos and words by
Hannah Armstrong

Hannah Coates is an illustrator and graphic designer, born and raised in Derry and now living in Belfast. Her work mixes landscapes with dreamscapes, bringing to life the space between fantasy and reality. Here she talks to Freckle *about her journey so far and dreams for the future.*

Tell us about how you came to be the artist you are today.

From no age I always wanted to draw. I thought it was great when I was younger that there was a school just for people who painted all day! As I was growing up, I wanted to be an artist – then a fashion designer, then a costume designer, then a textile designer. I went to the University of Ulster and did Textile Design, but it wasn't what I expected. Then I did Visual Communication in my Foundation Year – it was a bit of everything, and I realised that illustration and design work was what I wanted to do.

Your artwork is colourful, layered and fantastical ... how do you create this effect?

I start drawing with pen, colour it in with inks or paints and then scan each bit into Photoshop, bringing them all together. People when they look at my sketchbooks are like, "Where's that drawing?" Well, here's a little bit, and here's another bit! I have never thrown away a sketchbook in my life; I look back at my work and take some elements from it. It's an awkward way of working but I find it works best for me.

Your work was used by the band and fellow Derry-natives Sullivan and Gold for their tour posters. How did that come about?

It was sheer accident, really – and meant to happen. There's a company called Dog Ears in Derry who do publishing for children's books and e-books. I sent them a link to my website, and they forwarded it to their Graphic Design office. It got forwarded on again to Smalltown America Records, who'd signed Sullivan and Gold, so the band saw my stuff and were like, "Will you do a poster for us?" And I was like, "Yeah!!" They were going on tour to Scotland, so I started looking up the Isle of Skye, the mountains – bleak, but bright as well.

Mountains are a common feature in your collection, Moonrise Kingdom. *Are there any landscapes in Northern Ireland that you particularly enjoy or find inspiration in?*

I have to go over the Glenshane Pass to get home, and always when I see it I think,

>>

"Aw, I'm nearly home!" It's always really lovely, especially with the heather that's growing – some years it would make the whole landscape purple.

What are you working on at the minute?

The London Illustration Fair is a four-day event in December where they select illustrators from all over the UK to exhibit their work, and I got picked for it! I actually rang up my mum,

like, tears of joy running down my face. I've got so much work to do, I'm drawing as much as I can as fast as I can. The work is actually my dad's idea – he said, "I had this dream where you drew the Himalayas, and little Tibetan monasteries all over it." I thought, "That's actually a really nice idea, usually your ideas are terrible!" I want to make it big, something with a lot of impact. It's going to be crazy but I'm looking forward to it.

What do you see for yourself in the future?

I definitely see myself being an artist for the rest of my life. It's funny because I can't see myself doing anything else. I really want to learn screen printing; if I got really good at it I could set up my own space to do screen printing – that's the dream.

What message would you like to share with your audience?

It's OK not to have everything as it should be. Do it from your own imagination. Don't worry about making it perfect. Being surreal is actually nicer to look at. Insanity is more interesting than sanity. ●

CREATIVITY IS POWERFUL

photo and words by Journeyfor

Imagine your life right now suddenly coming to a standstill, a crossroads. You have made bad choices and ended up with nothing. You wonder how you got here, how the equation of your life has added up to this.

Your story, if it was told, would be difficult reading. Like most, you have had hardship but at those times perhaps your way of dealing with it was to step back into the dark shadow of a substance: heroin, alcohol, ketamine, cocaine, valium. For some the decline is slow and creeps unnoticed into their lives, for others it is a violent, adrenaline-fueled sprint towards oblivion and destruction.

Addiction is a strange animal that comes to live in you and with you, moulding itself to your individuality, making your struggle unique. When you finally try to extract yourself the hold is too strong, the desire too driven.

This is the experience of some of the residents of Carlisle House, a rehabilitation and treatment centre nestled in the heart of Belfast off the Antrim Road, at the foot of Cave Hill. For the past two years Journeyfor, a creative agency from Belfast, have been running story making sessions at the residential unit.

If you looked in on the one-and-a-half-hour workshop on a Thursday afternoon you might see people acting passionately, drawing intensely or studying a wall of post-it notes all documenting individual moments of clarity or heartfelt and honest insights into their experiences of living with addiction. There is one thing that unites the group and that is the desire to understand and explore their own unique story through creativity.

Who likes to see their own image, to study it, to de-construct it, to take it apart? We all find it hard when, through circumstance or necessity, we find ourselves in the limelight. However, the initial recoil and squirming usually subsides and gives way to fascination and intrigue, we observe ourselves moving, talking, 'do I really look like that', 'is that how the back of my head looks?' Most of us will never appear on film, although in this age of image transfer, selfies and immediate upload more of us are seeing ourselves through shared image. This shift in how we share and entertain ourselves is having a major effect on how we communicate, interact and more importantly how we see our own self-image.

Journeyfor uses film in the residential unit in a very different way. Residents are encouraged to talk on film about their experiences and then watch these very personal and honest clips of their own stories with other members of the group. This has a strange and transforming effect on everyone involved. It provides distance and perspective, a mirroring of their immediate circumstances that can sometimes be too much to take, but at the same time powerful and revealing. While watching themselves residents have expressed feelings of anxiety, embarrassment and fascination, but above all, healing. These unique films are facilitated by Journeyfor but made by the group members. They are created with a minimal amount of editing as a crucial part of the process is to stay true to the motivation - to be an honest statement.

For some, having never considered writing or film making in their lives as something powerful or transforming, this process is a revelation. The act of committing their stories to paper or screen becomes an important step towards getting clean. •

ECHO ECHO

*photos by Sarah Bryden Photography
and Living Witness Productions
words by Anna-Marie McAlinden*

Echo Echo Dance Theatre Company was created by Steve Batts and the late Ursula Laeubli in Amsterdam in 1991. After six years of project work touring in Europe, it relocated to Derry, Northern Ireland. One of the most exciting developments in the Company's recent history and a realisation of a long-term dream occurred in April 2013 when Echo Echo moved into its new home.

Most echoes reflect off walls – but Echo Echo's stunning new home is literally subsumed within Derry's Historic City Walls. Anyone lucky enough to visit Echo Echo's premises will understand its passion for this new space immediately. As well as being well-equipped, bright and modern with stunning panoramic views over the City and beyond, the space is simply beautiful. Fertile ground indeed for vibrant creativity.

This new centre for dance and movement art is where the Company lives, works, creates and grows – it is also a place where the public and friends can connect, engage, collaborate and exchange ideas. And the benefits are quickly showing themselves, for Echo Echo's ensemble of local and international dancers have already produced an impressive body of work. Recent highlights include its extensive programme during Derry's City of Culture year, and its Festival of Dance and Movement performance (November 2014) which were received enthusiastically by the City and beyond.

But Echo Echo is even more than a world-class dance performance company – it also runs open classes for all ages and all abilities, and it plays an important role in the community through its extensive outreach work. One successful example would be the DCAL Creativity Month Project, where Echo Echo engaged with eight primary schools within walking distance of the dance centre.

The company has also created and supported other educational participatory projects with various partners, including a collaboration with the Workers' Educational Association (WEA) to produce the 'Body Wisdom' dance project for people aged fifty and over. 'Body Wisdom', which began in 2009, has now developed into one of Echo Echo's most popular weekly classes. It encourages creative poetic sensibility and helps participants to enjoy their physicality no matter how they consider themselves to be; fit, unfit, able-bodied or otherwise. The idea is to appreciate the depth and wisdom that comes with age, and to value the more purposeful, reflective, physical rhythms of those who are over fifty.　　　>>

Although the abilities of the participants may vary, the inclusive and welcoming philosophy at Echo Echo is summed up by Ayesha Mailey, Echo Echo Associate Artistic Director and long-term member of the ensemble: "We believe everyone can dance – the very first time we express ourselves is through movement as we kick and move in our mother's belly…At Echo Echo we believe everyone has the ability to be poetic in movement".

Echo Echo's main aim for the future is to build upon both its enthusiastic audience base and its passion for physical theatre. The Company wants to make its space even more active and more successful, giving both artists and the public a voice through dance: "We would just say to people, don't shut the door on dance. You're not going to love or even like all types of dance – just like you wouldn't necessarily love

" At Echo Echo we believe everyone has the ability to be poetic in movement "

or like all art, all books, all music or all films – but try to be open to giving it a go as you might just find that you love it."

And that is exactly what happened to Ayesha over eighteen years ago, and she has never looked back! •

explore more at: www.echoechodance.com

BRIGHTEN YOUR WINTER

recipe by Chelsea Marshall
photos by Chelsea Marshall and Terence Finnegan

Eating locally during Northern Ireland's winters can be tough. It's been months since plump berries and crisp apples filled our shelves, and it will be months before crunchy lettuces, cucumbers and French beans will return to our gardens. Instead of relying solely on potatoes, carrots and onions – the work horses of winter cooking – try looking a little deeper into your farmer's store house, and you'll find an excellent source of colour and flavour to brighten your plates in the darker months.

Pumpkins and winter squashes, such as butternut, Crown Prince, acorn and Red Kuri, can be stored for many months and are a welcome source of nutrients and variety. Without too much effort, winter squashes can be roasted and added to soups, curries, pasta sauces, scones and baked treats for depth in either savoury or sweet dishes. You can also roast, purée and freeze small portions of the squash during the autumn to have handy portions available to bulk up or add colour to meals throughout the winter.

Galettes are free-form tarts that provide an easy base for your favourite sweet or savoury fillings any time of year. Talk to your local farmers to find out what is in season and try piling these combinations into your galette:

> *Spring*: asparagus, wild garlic,
> goat's cheese and Parmesan

> *Summer*: mixed ripe tomatoes,
> shallots and basil over a layer of
> feta cheese

> *Autumn*: apple, blackberry and
> cinnamon sugar

I have included a crust recipe that works well here – you want something buttery and flaky to contrast the depth of the filling – but feel free to use one you're most comfortable with. For sweet galettes, replace the pepper with a small amount of sugar.

" try looking a little deeper into your farmer's store house, and you'll find an excellent source of colour and flavour to brighten your plates in the darker months "

WINTER SQUASH &
BLUE CHEESE GALETTE

Preparation time 45 minutes
Total time 2.5 hours
Serves 6 with a salad or 8-10 as a starter

For the crust

175g flour (or mixture of wholemeal
and white), more for dusting
Salt and pepper
115g butter (very cold, diced)
1 large egg, beaten
Very cold water
Spoonful of milk
Optional: 30g hazelnuts, toasted and
chopped finely

For the filling

1 small butternut squash (500-600g)
1 medium onion
2-3 sprigs thyme
Olive oil or rapeseed oil
Salt and Pepper
50g blue cheese, chopped or crumbled
Optional: Roasted and chopped
hazelnuts/pecans, sprinkled on
top just before serving

1. Place flour, salt and pepper in a medium bowl and add diced butter. Combine flour and butter with a fork or use your hands to mix until you have course crumbs. Add egg and mix gently until mixture just comes together (do not over mix, as you want pockets of butter to remain). Add chopped hazelnuts if using and only as much ice-cold water as you need to form a loose ball. Place dough in cling film, form a disc and chill in the refrigerator for at least an hour (up to overnight).

2. About 20 minutes before the dough is fully chilled, pre-heat the oven to 190°C and prepare your filling. Peel butternut squash and remove seeds and stringy insides. Cut in half lengthwise and slice into thin rounds or half-moons (no more than 1/2 cm wide). Slice onion thinly and combine with squash and 2 spoonfuls of olive/rapeseed oil in a medium mixing bowl. Season with salt, pepper and the leaves from the sprigs of thyme. Mix until evenly coated and set aside.

3. Line a sheet pan with greaseproof paper. On a floured surface, roll out dough in a rough circle until 1/2 cm thick. Move crust carefully to prepared pan and layer filling evenly on top, leaving a one-inch outer edge. Fold outer edge over the filling and secure by folding over itself. Lightly brush a spoonful of milk over exposed crust.

4. Bake in pre-heated oven for 45-55 minutes. After 20 minutes, check that the crust is browning evenly, and turn oven down to 170°C if getting too dark. The galette is ready when the crust is a deep golden and, more importantly, there is very little resistance when you pierce the squash with a fork. Five minutes before the galette is finished, sprinkle crumbled blue cheese over top and return to the oven to melt.

5. Serve directly from oven or at room temperature.

ANONYMOUS THANK YOUS

We asked a few of our supporters and contributors to write a mini thank you to someone or something that makes their life better. Northern Ireland is a small place, maybe you'll recognise a few.

To Rob & Paul,

Thank you for your inspiration, trust, understanding and enthusiasm - it has been life changing for us. "Many men follow the sea - but not many were born to it. You both were."

Fair winds and tides to you.

To Mum and Dad,

Thank you for seeding my love of forests, mountains, rivers and the wild.

Dear Seamus Heaney,

Thank you for your words. We miss you. Like you said, "if you have the words, there's always a chance that you'll find the way."

Thank you to all the humans in my life for your humanity.

Thanks to the blue sky, the oceans, the rivers and lakes.

Thanks to the forests and the lush greenery of this earth.

You make me smile.

Beth, Rami and Tim

Here's to Norté. "Being ahead of your time isn't easy: the world ridicules you, time passes, then they label the imitators, innovators. The future is now."

LL Cool J

You ...
Taught me to see the beauty and goodness in our natural world,
To find strength and hope in the ebb and flow of the tide,
To hear the birds.
Introduced me to the mountains and snow.
Told me I would love again when I believed I never could

Thank you.

Vincy and Veronica (mum & dad),

Thanks for welcoming me back home when I needed a home most. Thanks for listening, for the lovely breakfasts, the coffee in my car, the ironed clothes, the hugs first thing in the morning and last thing at night.

I love you both x

THE FACTS OF LIFE

Pádraig Ó Tuama

That you were born
and you will die.

That you will sometimes love enough
and sometimes not.

That you will lie
if only to yourself.

That you will get tired.

That you will learn most from the situations
you did not choose.

That there will be some things that move you
more than you can say.

That you will live
that you must be loved.

That you will avoid questions most
urgently in need of your attention.

That you began as the fusion of a sperm and an egg
of two people who once were strangers
and may well still be.

That life isn't fair.

That life is sometimes good
and sometimes even better than good.

That life is often not so good.

That life is real
and if you can survive it, well,
survive it well,
with love
and art
and meaning given
where meaning's scarce.

That you will learn to live with regret.
That you will learn to live with respect.

That the structures that constrict you
may not be permanently constraining.

That you will probably be okay.

That you must accept change
before you die
but you will die anyway.

So you might as well live
and you might as well love.

You might as well love.
You might as well love.

Taken from Pádraig Ó Tuama's *Sorry for your Troubles*, Canterbury Press 2013

EXPLORING

"Sail forth – steer for the deep waters only,
Reckless O soul, exploring, I with thee, and thou with me,
For we are bound where mariner has not yet dared to go,
And we will risk the ship, ourselves and all."

Passage to India, *Walt Whitman*

WILD PLACES

Freckle *asked two professional photographers to share some of their favourite wild places in Northern Ireland*

« previous page

DOWNHILL BEACH

Tony Pleavin

This beach is wide and long; open to the elements, it feels like you're on the edge of the world. When the wind is blowing, waves breaking and the clouds are flying by, it just lifts the soul.

above

BEARNAGH

Simon Mills

I love the view from Slieve Bearnagh. I think it's my favourite of the Mourne Mountains. The ascents from all directions are great climbs and the views from the top are spectacular. It's also one of my favourite places to camp too, exposed yet sheltered by those mighty tors.

» opposite

TOLLYMORE FOREST

Simon Mills

When I first moved to Northern Ireland one of the first places I was taken to was Tollymore Forest. Although the snow wasn't as heavy as it is in these shots it was still the depths of winter, the trees were frosted and I could see the Mournes rising above in the distance and I knew I wanted to get out there and explore.

OXFORD ISLAND

Tony Pleavin

I've been photographing this jetty for over ten years; always pre-dawn and it just keeps drawing me back. You're not far from civilisation but the Lough has such tranquillity you could be miles from anywhere. I will never tire of this place.

FELLOW BIKES

Ormeau Road, Belfast
photos by Gavin Millar
words by Lynn Finnegan

―――――――――

"We like to think every bike has a story. That story could be anything from a race-winning champion to someone who loved their bike dearly and rode it to work everyday. We are continuing that story, using the bare bones of old bikes and bringing them to life again."

―――――――――

You build bikes for people by using the bare bones of an old bike and breathing new life into it. Tell us more.

We build new bikes using old bicycle frames, restored and newly painted, and then build up the bike with new components. Our customers get a new bike but also a beautiful piece of history literally at its centre. We like to think we can help continue the story, rather than that old bike frame ending up in a skip or someone's shed for fifty years. A lot of what we do harks back to a bygone age of cycling before carbon and composites and all this kind of stuff, where it was just steel frames and really simple. That is what we're trying to achieve.

And you are situated on the Ormeau Road in Belfast, a place that also has a lot of history.

We love where we live and work, and want to be good neighbours. We want to see the Ormeau road be a community, because it can be divided in so many ways. Bikes can help bring life to it. Kids come in looking for their chains to be fixed, and we've recently built a trendy fixy for a nineteen-year-old alongside a single speed and touring bike for a newly retired couple planning their next big adventure. We're not saying we're Utopia, but our vision is to be more than just a bike shop – we want to be a community hub.

Does this ever feel difficult?

It's hard to say without sounding terribly pompous and idealistic, but we always said to each other we would be the type of business that value people over profit. It's easy to get caught up in the daily grind of deadlines, so the biggest challenge has been staying true to ourselves and sticking with this vision.

It sounds like you have been thinking about this for a long time.

The idea has been there for a long, long time. We started out fixing up bikes in our back gardens, and sometimes the kitchen table if we weren't caught. The three of us (Patrick, Jon and Elder) got to the stage where it was obvious we all really wanted to fully commit to it. We spent a while dreaming about what it would be like to have actual premises. I remember the night we were having a pint in the Errigle and we saw these grey doors across the road and were like, 'I wonder what's in there'. We contacted the landlord somehow and ended up moving in. We gave it a name, and Fellow officially opened its doors in August 2013.

All three of you are keen cyclists and always planning your next weekend ride or week-long trip away. Where would you recommend we take a bike ride if we had a free Sunday afternoon?

There's a route that is around eighty miles where you can head down to Comber on the Comber Greenway, and then head on down to Strangford and get the ferry across to Portaferry. There's a lovely little cafe in Portaferry that does amazing pancakes and coffee, perfect after forty miles. After refueling you can cycle back over the

peninsula to absolutely breathtaking views. I've been down there in every weather condition and the views are always totally worth it. (If you want to find out more, find a copy of Fellow Gazette, Volume One, in cafes or on their website.)

Or if you're feeling more relaxed, head out along the Lagan towpath early in the morning to spend some time along the river. You can turn around whenever you need to, so it's perfect for a last-minute escape or to squeeze in a much-needed dose of fresh air.

What is your vision for cycling in Northern Ireland in the next five to ten years?

We would love people to see the value in cycling, to see that it is more than just a sport. It can be not just an acceptable means of transport, but one that is better for our fitness, mental health, the environment and personal finances. I wish people could see that. But I think it comes hand in hand with our society and road users becoming more accepting of cyclists, which might only come with a solid infrastructure that is clearly marked out and obeyed.

If there was one thing about bikes that you would want everyone to know, what would it be?

That more people would remember how much fun it was to ride a bike when they were a kid. Even if it's raining. Sometimes this is forgotten. Most people had a bike when they were young, and loved it. It doesn't need to be any different now. •

explore more at: www.fellowbicycleco.com

THE HIDDEN VISION

Traffic-free greenways and cycle routes have long been celebrated for their contribution to our quality of life. They're a no-brainer: they're better for health, well-being, our financial bills, national carbon reduction targets and getting us out into the fresh air without feeling in danger from other traffic.

Northern Ireland has a small handful of traffic-free greenways, but compared to the rest of Europe we are, frankly, kind of embarrassing ourselves. Tens of thousands of miles of high quality cycle routes like Eurovelo cover the continent, serving the desire of people from around the world to embark on epic cycling holidays.

Less than 1% of our children cycle to school, compared to almost 50% in Denmark and the Netherlands. We struggle to fit expensive trips to the gym into our daily routines, while we could be staying healthy by travelling under our own power for most day-to-day trips we make. In a country where 44% of households in the capital city have no access to a car, why are we not fully embracing the greenway movement?

The well-loved active travel blog, Northern Ireland Greenways, provides a vision of cycling infrastructure which could provide safe space for commuters, families and adventurers alike. It incorporates a web of forgotten railways that lie dormant throughout some of Northern Ireland's most beautiful landscapes. These abandoned routes link villages, towns, cities, workplaces and visitor attractions; crumbling relics of a proud engineering heritage lost to time, which could once again form an economic, tourism and transport backbone of Northern Ireland. Imagine over six hundred miles of traffic-free paths ... •

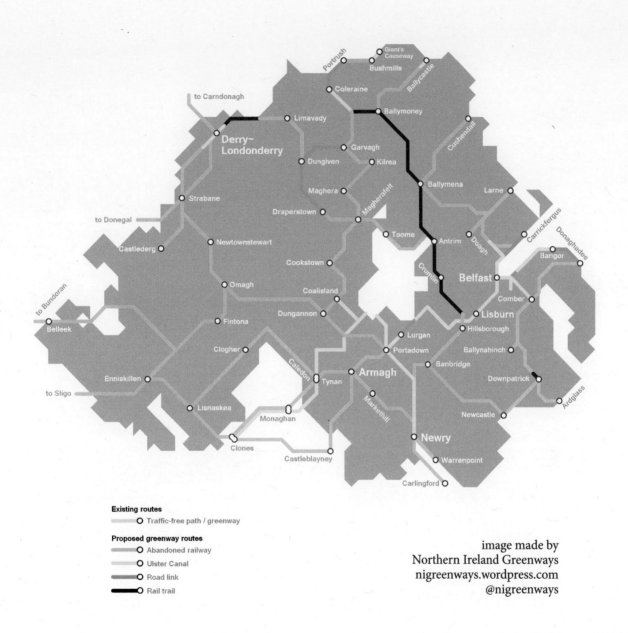

Portrush
Giant's
Causeway
Bushmills
Ballycastle
Coleraine
to Carndonagh
Limavady
Ballymoney
Cushendall
Derry~
Londonderry
Garvagh
Dungiven
Kilrea
Maghera
Ballymena
Larne
Strabane
Draperstown
Magherafelt
to Donegal
Toome
Antrim
Doagh
Carrickfergus
Donaghadee
Castlederg
Newtownstewart
Cookstown
Crumlin
Belfast
Bangor
to Bundoran
Omagh
Coalisland
Comber
Belleek
Dungannon
Lisburn
Fintona
Lurgan
Hillsborough
Clogher
Portadown
Ballynahinch
Downpatrick
Enniskillen
Caledon
Armagh
Banbridge
to Sligo
Tynan
Markethill
Ardglass
Lisnaskea
Newcastle
Monaghan
Newry
Clones
Castleblayney
Warrenpoint
Carlingford

Existing routes

○ Traffic-free path / greenway

Proposed greenway routes

○ Abandoned railway
○ Ulster Canal
○ Road link
○ Rail trail

image made by
Northern Ireland Greenways
nigreenways.wordpress.com
@nigreenways

PARKOUR

Exploring urban terrain

Nestled in Belfast's Titanic Quarter, T13 is a haven for parkour, BMXing and urban adventuring. Paul Allen is twenty four, born and raised in Magherafelt and travels to T13 nearly every day on his motorbike.

photos by Rebecca McMaster
words by Ben Craig

First of all, what is Parkour?

"Parkour is an urban sport, moving freely through, over, round or under any terrain using your body. It challenges you physically and mentally and it helps with social development because there is complete freedom of expression. Everyone has their own style and comes up with their own way to overcome an obstacle. Anybody at any age can do it: you don't need to be a gymnast."

Why do you travel to T13?

"It's the opportunities in Urban Sports that pulls me back. T13 does everything from break dancing, skateboarding, rollerblading, parkour and a gym, to even music nights. It's an amazing place, with such a fun and friendly vibe. It used to be that the different urban sports wouldn't mix but now we are all together under one roof so the skateboarders hang out with the rollerbladers or BMXers and that would never have happened maybe 10 years ago. I just love it, the variety, the people and the experience."

How did you first get involved?

"I first came to T13 four years ago when I was 20. I came because I was looking for somewhere to rollerblade, so it was nothing to do with Parkour. I never thought I would end up coaching Parkour, I just gave it a go for fun. About a year later I was down in Dublin for a competition called Kings of Concrete, where I met the owners of T13, Liam Lynch & Matt Gillespie. It was a fun competition and a good chance to hang out with the community from Northern Ireland and Southern Ireland together. Liam and Matt asked me if I'd run a few Parkour workshops at T13, I said yes, started working with youth groups and loved it."

Tell us about the groups you work with.

"They are from all different communities and backgrounds. They often get involved because it gives them an opportunity they don't have in their own area, but it also brings people together. I have a few Autistic students who, when they first came, found it really difficult even to look at me, they were getting in trouble in their communities for raking about and nothing seemed to capture their interest. I got to know them, built relationships with them, demonstrated some big moves like a standing backflip and suddenly I had their attention. We built a bond and now their coordination, strength and ability to talk with others have all improved and they are fully integrated in my programme. I have about 50 people who come every week and it's great to see them all progress and have a lot of fun together."

Where has Parkour taken you?

"It's been awesome. I've met so many people from all over the world including some from Lisses in France where Parkour originated and I've met one of the co-founders of Parkour, Sébastien Foucan. I train a lot, including 2-3 gym sessions a week, and am very careful about nutrition. I'm now starting my own business called Jump NI where I can bring Parkour to people in their communities and take my work on the road. Not everyone likes to play the mainstream sports like rugby, football, GAA, netball or hockey so I think it's really important to give those young people other opportunities like this so that they can build their confidence, meet new people and get out of the house or off the street corner." ●

" ... there is complete freedom of expression. Everyone has their own style and comes up with their own way to overcome an obstacle. "

Explore more at: www.t13.tv and www.jumpni.co.uk

TEN FOUNDATIONS

photos by Connor Tilson
words by Mick McEvoy

"Tell me, what is it you plan to do
with your one wild and precious life?"

Mary Oliver

Life is full of remarkable people. Ian Campbell from Newcastle, Co. Down is one of them. Ian and his wife Evie lost their home, their life savings and their business all in the same year he was diagnosed with prostate cancer. They went through very difficult times during Ian's illness, but he has been given a clean bill of health and sees life through the eyes of someone who has been given a second chance. He has explored the world and made a decision about how he is going to live in it.

With this second chance he decided to help others. Ian established a charity called TEN Foundations, a non-religious charity working to ensure homeless and vulnerable children living in the Philippines have the chance to grow up in a safe and loving environment. The charity has also created a *Sustainable Livelihoods* project, working with local women in communities across the Philippines.

Ian is now responsible for raising £500 per week to ensure that over two hundred children are fed and cared for and the *Sustainable Livelihoods* project is also supported. "I do feel the pressure sometimes, but it's a good pressure. I have always thought about doing something like a building project with Habitat for Humanity or some other charity. With my experience I knew I could do it but it was never the right time or there was always some excuse. Well, now is the time!"

Originally based in a shop on the promenade in Newcastle, TEN Foundations can now be found on the Lisburn Road in Belfast. Entering the shop you'll be greeted with a welcoming smile from Ian himself or one of the many volunteers, cosy mismatched sofas, vintage clothing, handmade crafts and the smell of freshly-brewed coffee. Due to the economic downturn Ian has been able to secure a large retail unit for TEN

>>

> " I do feel the pressure sometimes, but it's a good pressure. I have always thought about doing something like a building project with Habitat for Humanity ... but it was never the right time or there was always some excuse. Well, now is the time! "

Foundations rent-free, enabling every penny to go to his projects in the Philippines. With help from Duncan, Derek and Tony – carpenter, joiner and electrician by trade – they got to work fitting out the shop, using reclaimed wooden pallets to make almost all of the chairs, sofas and shelving you see when you walk in.

The shop is full of amazing products made by skilled women in communities across the Philippines. With old sewing machines, used packaging such as rice sacks (that would normally be thrown away) are transformed into handbags and rucksacks. Disposable plastic drinking straws are flattened and woven to make shopping bags and pencil cases. This investment in local women's skills and livelihoods builds their capacity to sustain themselves, their families and their communities.

"The thing that motivates me the most are my three grandchildren," says Ian. "I only have to imagine them living the way these children in the Philippines have to. When I tuck my grandchildren in at night and whisper in their ear 'I love you', to know that those babies and children never feel that security, it just tears me apart. They just need a cuddle, a kind word, a warm meal, a safe place to call home and to know that for once in their short lives that someone cares."

Ian and the team have already transformed the lives of many children and adults in the Philippines, and seem full of energy to keep going. They host regular fundraising events, from fashion shows and bake offs to live music and 'Mindful Movie' nights. Browsing their beautiful handcrafted products feels like you are exploring another corner of the world: a solid link to people in another continent, fairly traded and to be treasured. The last word goes to Ian, this remarkable man: "I'm the happiest I've ever been." ●

explore more at: www.tenfoundations.org
NEXT PAGE: Ian with two of the volunteers, and the shop on Lisburn Road, Belfast

WHAT ARE YOU THINKING?

This is Freckle's first issue: we still have lots to learn and we always
like to hear from people. If you have any stories you think would
be good in Freckle, anything you think we can improve,
or you would like to contribute to future issues,
please get in touch.

CONTACT

www.frecklenorthernireland.org
twitter: @freckleni
facebook: facebook.com/frecklenorthernireland
email: freckleni@gmail.com